# THE
# WEAPONS
## OF OUR
# WARFARE

### LIVING VICTORIOUSLY
### IN JESUS CHRIST

## DANIEL AGUILAR

# DEDICATION

To Revive Youth in Hillsboro, Oregon. I received the inspiration to write this book, because of the Holy Spirit and the teenagers in that group.

## Special Thanks To:

God, for restoring my creativity and for giving me this newly found passion to write.

My wife Sonja, for being so strong and for walking alongside me throughout this entire journey.

Pastor Keely of East River Fellowship, for prophesying this book into existence.

Pastor Chase of East River Fellowship, for helping me make this book possible.

Everyone who encouraged me to write this book.

# TABLE OF CONTENTS

# INTRODUCTION

* * *

"Daniel, did you leave the sprinklers on?" "No dad." I replied. "Then what is that noise in the backyard?" My dad and I went out back to check. We saw our two dogs barking by the tall cypress trees that lined our backyard wall. As we approached our dogs, we noticed a big rattlesnake! His tail was up in the air, rattling, and making a noise that was as loud as a sprinkler system. It was warning my dogs to stay back. My dad looked at me, "Daniel, hand me that weed wacker wire." Then my dad grabbed a long metal pole. My dad looped the wire through the metal pole and made a noose out of it on one end. He said, "Daniel, I am going to put this noose around the snakes neck, and when I say pull, then I need you to pull and not let go. Got it!" "Got it!" I replied. So we inched closer to the snake and its rattler became even louder. Suddenly I hear, "pull!" So I pulled the wire as tight as I could and my dad had caught the snake! He then helped me bring it from behind the trees onto our patio. The snake was flailing frantically. We had a wooden cover over our patio, so he had me hold the snake up to one of the wooden beams that held up the cover. My dad grabbed a large nail and a hammer and pounded the nail right through the snakes head! He grabbed a big knife and chopped its head off and the snakes body hit the ground. The body was still moving, but the snake was dead.

*Is this not a picture of Father, Son and Holy Spirit destroying the enemy and his works?*

I remember the fear that welled up in me that day as a nine year old. I was scared my dogs would get bit and die. I was scared that my dad would get bit and die. The experience didn't make me want to play outside again, even though I loved playing outside as a child. There was construction taking place in a big field not too far from our house. That's how the snake got in our backyard in the first place. I was afraid it would happen again. But, I also learned something else that day. I learned that though there was a problem, there was a solution. I learned that I had a father who had a plan to save me; a father who asked his son to help fulfill that plan. I also learned that in order to have peace in my life and around my home, the snake had to be defeated. Can you see where I am going with this?

The snake is the devil. Revelation 12:9 and Genesis 3:1 makes that clear. My dad is the Father who had a solution. Genesis 3:15 and John 3:16 make that clear. The nail that went through the snake, symbolizes the nails that went through Jesus. Acts 10:38-40 speaks to that.

That snake in our backyard, much like the devil, wants to instill fear in us. He wants to take residence in our heart and home and hinder us from living a full life in Jesus Christ (John 10:10). But, the devil was defeated! Hebrews 2:14-15 says, *"Inasmuch then as the children have partaken of flesh and blood, He Himself likewise shared in the same, that through death He might destroy him who had the power of death, that is the devil, and release those who through fear of death were all their lifetime subject to bondage."* The outcome is that we are released from fear of death. But why would anyone be afraid of death, other than the sheer fear of the unknown? Because people are afraid to die in their sins (Ephesians 2), and being separated from God for eternity. But there is a solution!

Galatians 2:20 says, "*I have been crucified with Christ; it is no longer I who live, but Christ lives in me; and the life which I now live in the flesh I live by faith in the Son of God, who loved me and gave Himself for me.*" All the evil, junk, darkness, sin and everything else that separated us from God has been taken care of on the cross! (Colossians 2:13-15). When I gave my life to Christ at 20 years old, I could see that memory of the snake being nailed to that wooden beam. It was taken care of. No longer able to roam about freely and instill fear in me or my family. It was dead, just like my old life and all because Jesus paid the price for me!

Even though I have given my life to Jesus Christ, why do I still struggle? Though the War has been won, why do I seem to fight so many battles of faith everyday? I thought I was set free? The truth is that I am set free. But the other truth is that I still have to battle the enemy. Why? Because we are still in a war.

## What war?

"*And war broke out in heaven: Michael and his angels fought with the dragon; and the dragon and his angels fought, but they did*

12

*not prevail, nor was a place found for them in heaven any longer. So the great dragon was cast out, that serpent of old, called the Devil and Satan, who deceives the whole world; he was cast to the earth, and his angels were cast out with him. Then I heard a loud voice saying in heaven, 'Now salvation, and strength, and the kingdom of our God, and the power of His Christ have come, for the accuser of our brethren, who accused them before our God day and night, has been cast down. And they overcame him by the blood of the Lamb and by the word of their testimony, and they did not love their lives to the death. Therefore rejoice, O heavens, and you who dwell in them!* **Woe to the inhabitants of the earth and the sea! For the devil has come down to you, having great wrath, because he knows that he has a short time.'"**

– REVELATION 12:7-12

The enemy has been defeated! But now he makes war with those who belong to God. Revelation 20 gives the end result of the enemies fate, but until that time, 1 Peter 5:8-9 makes it clear that the enemy is still roaming about this earth, taking down whoever he can.

The enemy will attack us strategically and he doesn't play fair. He goes for our weak spots. Whether he attacks us with persecution from another Christian, sensual thoughts, nightmares, fear, anxiety, depression, loneliness, anger, lies, etc. You can literally feel the spiritual oppression come upon you and it does hinder our walk and fellowship with God. It slows us down in our faith journey. (Read Daniel 10 for clarification) It can even turn people away from following after God all together. *Though the attacks of the enemy are real and heavy, so is the solution.*

## WHAT'S THE SOLUTION?

Jesus has given us weapons to fight off the attacks of the enemy.

*"For though we walk in the flesh, **we do not war according to the flesh. For the weapons of our warfare are not carnal but mighty in God** for pulling down strongholds, casting down arguments and every high thing that exalts itself against the knowledge of God, bringing every thought into captivity to*

14

*the obedience of Christ, and being ready to punish all disobedience when your obedience is fulfilled."*

- 2 Corinthians 10:3-6

Spiritual attacks require spiritual weapons! We will discover and apply seven weapons in this book. Before we dive into them, let's take a moment to understand what the weapons of God are capable of doing.

### THE WEAPONS OF GOD DO THE FOLLOWING:

1. *Pulls down strongholds.* A stronghold is a fortress and firm stand against. In football, a defensive player known as a cornerback, is meant to guard the offensive player known as a wide receiver. The cornerback is aloud to press and push the wide receiver as much as he wants within five yards of the line of scrimmage (where the ball is set and hiked from). The cornerback would try to jam the wide receiver at the line, or push him out of bounds to make him ineligible for that play. The cornerback was not supposed to do this, but he would grab the jersey of the wide receiver

to slow him down. This is how a stronghold of the enemy can be. It is something that has power and control over your life. These can include addictions, low self esteem, depression, anxiety, etc. But these strongholds can be broken!

I played wide receiver on my football team. My older brother taught me a move to free me from the cornerback. He taught me to smack his hands away. Sometimes, I would have to smack the cornerbacks hands extremely hard. This made him not want to grab my jersey again. Sounds intense, but it worked. It made the cornerback give me space so I could run my passing route more freely. The same principle applies towards the enemy. When put into action, the spiritual weapons of God free us from the enemy's strongholds. Once free, we are able to run God's "route" for our lives without hindrance!

2. *Bring every thought into captivity to the obedience of Christ.* (This refers to the lying thoughts, which are in direct opposition to the truth of God). I loved to draw pictures as a

kid. I was born in 1990 and enjoyed Pokémon. I had a poster of the original 150 Pokémon and I drew all of them in my art pad! I continued drawing throughout my teenage years. Then I was introduced to drugs and began to draw while under the influence. I began to draw better than I ever had. But, my pictures began to turn dark and evil in their meanings. Then I met Jesus and He set me free from my addiction! But I noticed that I had no desire to draw anymore. I believed the lie, that if I was not under the influence of drugs, then I wasn't capable of drawing good pictures. For the next 7 years, I did not draw a single picture.

One day, I was spending time with Jesus and I heard Holy Spirit say to me, "I want you to draw again!" I replied, "I don't know what to draw." Holy Spirit said, "I will show you." I began to weep uncontrollably. I told this to my wife and she surprised me with an early Christmas present; an art set! I drew a picture for her for Christmas. It was my first drawing in 7 years! Then I drew her another picture for the following Christmas. Those two pictures are currently hanging on the walls in our home. Honestly, they are the best pictures that I have ever drawn. The only influence I was under, was that of the Holy Spirit! God gave me my creativity back.

Before I started drawing again I had this brief conversation with God. I said to God, "I'm sorry God, but I'm not creative." He replied, "That is impossible. I am creative and you are made in My image! So, how can you not be creative?" (Genesis 1-2). The weapons of God allow us to grab hold of lying thoughts. We are then able to bring them to God and in His power alone, He discards of them for us. In exchange for the lie, God gives us His truth. When the enemy said to me that I could never draw again, God spoke the truth and said, "the enemy can't steal the gifts I have given you!" (Romans 11:29). Thank you Lord for your truth and gift of art to me. With God's weapons, we are able to match every lie with the truth from God. The weapons of God are more powerful than the weapons of the enemy!

## So why are we being attacked?

Because the enemy is trying to topple the knowledge of God that we have. He is sending everything from his arsenal of hell to destroy our life in Christ. If we didn't have the knowledge of God (relationship) and we didn't have the knowledge of who we are in Christ (our true identity), then we wouldn't even be a threat to the enemy (Colossians 3:9-10). But, now we are on opposing teams to the enemy; thanks be to Jesus. The enemy doesn't like that too much. But, I don't care about the enemy. What I care about is living victoriously in this new life that Jesus Christ has given me. I care about you living the fullest life that God has for you as well!

## How do we live victoriously in Christ?

We have to know the arsenal of Heaven and what weapons are made available to us. But, knowledge is not enough. We have to know how to use our heavenly weapons properly or else they will remain idle. If we don't use these weapons, then we will continue to get beat on by the enemy. If we fight these spiritual battles in our own strength, then we will lose. But if we fight in the Lord's strength and do things His way, we will have victory.

> *"Now thanks be to God who always leads us in triumph in Christ, and through us diffuses the fragrance of His knowledge in every place."*
>
> - 2 CORINTHIANS 2:14

Let's dive in and see what are the weapons of our warfare!

# WEAPON ONE
## THANKFULNESS

* * *

What inspired me to write this book actually came from a sermon series I taught to my high school youth group. I kept hearing them talk about how much they were spiritually struggling. They would pray, read the Bible, go to church, talk to other people, but still no breakthrough. The most common struggle I kept hearing them talk about was anxiety. They would pray, but nothing would change. So I looked up the Scripture that talks about anxiety. Philippians 4:6-7 says, *"Be anxious for nothing, but in everything by prayer and supplication,* **with thanksgiving,** *let your requests be made known to God; and the* **peace of God,** *which surpasses all understanding, will guard your hearts and minds through Christ Jesus."*

The ingredient we were missing was thanksgiving! The peace of God will come, but we have to be thankful first. So before I began asking God for anything through prayer, I would simply thank God for what He has already given me. It looks something like this.

*"God, I thank you for giving me a new life. Thank you Jesus for laying down your life for mine. Thank you for delivering me from drug use. Thank you for my health. Thank you for allowing me to play sports. Thank you for helping me graduate college. Thank you for making me a pastor. Thank you for my wife. Thank you for putting a roof over my head. Thank you for giving my wife and I a car. Thank you for helping my wife graduate college. Thank you for safety."* And the list goes on and on.

Being thankful positions my heart accurately before God. It reminds me of God's goodness and faithfulness. It encourages me that God is my provider and He is always there for me. When I verbally list all that I am thankful for, it brings me peace like His Word promises. I begin to realize that I have much more than I thought I did. It helps me remember that God is the one that has given all of these things to me. It then gives me confidence to ask God to move in my life.

I know that it's very simple. It might even seem too elementary for some. But does it not say it right there in God's Word? Does it not say to be thankful and God's peace which surpasses all understanding will protect our hearts and minds?

Proverbs 4:23 says, *"Guard your heart with all diligence, for out of it spring the issues of life."* Anxiety, fear, depression, anger, lust...can all rule your life until you challenge them. Verbally stating what you are thankful for will fill your heart and will push out all the other things that don't belong there. Being thankful will bring you peace and will guard your heart and mind from anxiety.

### APPLICATION

What are you thankful for? Make a list and then verbally speak it out. Do this every day. Pick one or even multiple things that you are thankful for. When you feel anxiety or any other spiritual attack start to come against you, verbally state what you are thankful for.

A personal example: If a lie pops in your head that you are stupid, verbally speak about how you are thankful that you could even be accepted into college, let alone pass tests, read books, have deep conversations and then even graduate with a 3.29 gpa. That's after living a party lifestyle for years of your life and being the second person in your immediate family to graduate college. That's how we combat the enemy with thankfulness!

*"Continue earnestly in prayer, being vigilant in it with thanksgiving."*
- Colossians 4:2

Do you see how this works? There are weapons in our grasp to help us be victorious every day of our lives. We have to know what they are and how to use them. That's exactly what we are going to continue to do in this book.

**The first weapon of our warfare is thankfulness!**

# WEAPON TWO
## FORGIVENESS

* * *

When I was nine months old, my dad went to prison. He served eight years in Folsom prison for theft. My mom and dad met in Southern California, but when my dad got incarcerated, my mom moved my brother's, my sister, and I up to Folsom. During those eight years, my twin brother and I would go see my dad often. My mom worked the graveyard shift, so she could see my dad during the day visits. She would visit him whenever she had the chance. My dad was even given the opportunity for family visits. They had tiny apartment homes on the prison property where inmates could have their spouses and children stay a weekend with them. That means that husbands and wives could be intimate with each other during these visits. I am simply being real, because serving time in prison normally doesn't allow inmates those opportunities with their spouses. My dad was also able to see his twin boys.

It felt a little uncomfortable to be in a tiny two bedroom apartment surrounded by barbed wire. Most pieces to any games available were missing, so my brother and I had to use our imaginations. Or we would simply watch Barney and Power Rangers on the TV. It wasn't the most ideal set up, but my dad made the best of it. Most of the family visits had yards in them where my brother and I could catch lizards or look up at the stars at night. But, one family visit apartment had this cement back-yard that didn't allow in for any skylight view. As my twin brother and I had disappointed looks on our faces; concerned about what we were going to do for the weekend, my dad came up with a plan. He grabbed the empty Totino's pizza cartons that we ate for lunch earlier. Then he grabbed some tin foil and rolled it up in a ball. Then he grabbed Kool Aid packets and a newspaper and rolled that up. My dad made a baseball diamond with the mate-rials! My brother and I had a blast! We were so thankful that my dad made the best of every visit.

In the fall of 1999, my dad finally got out of prison. My mom bought a little two bedroom home so my dad had a place to himself when he got out.

She also bought him a truck that we nicknamed the "banana boat." It weighed a couple tons, it was dull yellow with a beige brown roof. It was an ugly truck that took 15 minutes to warm up every morning before you drove it or else it would break down on you. My brothers and I had to push it a few times. Nonetheless, it would get you from point A to point B. My mom thought my dad could use it for work. My dad lived with us for two years in that little home. This is the same home that I described in the introduction. But, the corruption in my dad's heart and the enemy playing off of my dad's weakness took him out. My dad committed adultery on my mom with the neighbor lady across the street. My mom is a believer and she tried working it out with my dad so they wouldn't have to get divorced. But my dad wanted his happiness and didn't want to be with my mom anymore. They were married for 34 years. My mom, twin brother, older brother and myself all moved up to Hillsboro Oregon in March 2002. I was 11 years old. My oldest sister lived in Hillsboro and she helped us get back on our feet.

I am telling this story from my childhood for a reason. My dad caused a lot of pain in my life. As I grew up, I kept asking myself and others this question, "How could my dad look at his twin boys and still want to leave?" Call me selfish, but I wasn't thinking about what was going on between my mom and dad's relationship. I was thinking about how my dad had twin boys that he could watch grow up and be involved in their lives. My dad missed all my school graduations, including my college graduation. My dad missed my pastoral ordination. My dad missed my wedding day. My wife is currently 6 months pregnant and my dad most likely won't see his grandchild. My twin brother has 4 kids of his own and my dad has never met them. How could he look at us, and not think about our lives he would miss out on? I didn't realize this truth until I was 27 years old. But when my dad walked out on us, I acquired a spirit of abandonment. I thought that I wasn't good enough for my dad.

The issue was, I did not realize that when I was a teenager, so my abandonment resulted into terrible actions. From the age of 13 to 20 years old, I participated in acts that attempted to fill the hole I didn't realize I had in my heart. I was introduced to pornography and masturbation at 12 years old. I then began to fool around with girls at 13 years old and eventually lost my virginity at 14 years old. I started smoking marijuana at 14 years old and I then took my first ecstasy pill when I was 16 years old. Not planning on taking ecstasy more than 7 times, I ended up going well over 200 pills before I decided to stop one day. I began to experiment with other drugs like cocaine and crystal meth before I became addicted to crystal meth for 5 years. The decisions that I made while on these substances devastated my entire being. I was destroying myself and I didn't even know why.

I will go into more detail about my faith journey in the next chapter, but the point of this chapter is to discuss the weapon of forgiveness. To make a long story short, on February 4th of 2011, I gave my life to Jesus! Immediately God set me free! My addiction to smoking cigarettes was broken, I broke up with my girlfriend, I stopped using drugs, I felt empowered and alive. The struggle was still real. It took me about 1 and a half years after I gave my life to Jesus to kick all addictions completely. Ephesians 4:23 says to be renewed in the spirit of our minds. I had just begun the transformation process. I had just begun my new life in Christ!

But the pivotal moment of forgiveness that changed everything for me took place in my kitchen at around 4am. I was working at Famous Footwear, stacking and sorting shoes all night when

God began to speak to me. He told me to leave everything behind. All the things that I just named above. I ended my shift, went to my house and began to cry out to God. I was confused how He could take someone like me and work through me for His purpose. I wasn't clear on what to do. Do I go to Oregon State and continue to live this life of sin? Or do I go to Multnomah and begin an entire new life that I know nothing about? Then I heard God's voice. He said, "You are going to Multnomah and you are going to be a pastor!" (More clarity on this story in the next chapter). I heard Him so clearly as if someone was in the room with me. I began to cry uncontrollably, and before I could even say thank you, the first words out of my mouth were, "I forgive my dad!"

In that moment I felt the weight of the world lift off my shoulders. I was forgiven by God for every horrible and evil act and thought that I have ever committed; past, present and future. God forgave me for everything! Washed clean and made brand new right on the spot. (Ephesians 1:13-14). So why were those the first words out of my mouth? Because my dad was the one who hurt me the most out of anyone else in this entire world. When I felt God forgive me for everything I have ever done,

I couldn't help but forgive my dad for everything that he had ever done. I was set free! I have never been the same since.

You have heard it said, "forgive but don't forget." But, the Bible tells us to forgive and forget. Why? Because that's what God does with us and our sins. He forgives us and forgets all of our sins. How can He forget when He is the all knowing God? He chooses to forget our sins. Now that's a loving God!

In Jeremiah 31:34 God says, *"For I will forgive their iniquity, and their sin I will remember no more."*

In Isaiah 43:25 God says, *"I, even I, am He who blots out your transgressions for My own sake; and I will not remember your sins."*

In Psalm 103:12 God says, *"As far as the east is from the west, so far has He removed our transgressions from us."*

How is it possible to forgive others completely and then totally forget what they have done to you? That seems unjust and outright unfair. But let me ask you this: What has God forgiven you for? Think about all the junk you have done. Every thought and action, yet God forgave you for all of it; past, present and future! This is why God says in

Ephesians 4:32 - "*And be kind to one another, tenderhearted, forgiving one another, even as God in Christ forgave you.*" Now I am not saying that it is easy. I am not saying that that makes the situation okay. I talked to my dad on the phone at 27 years old. When I finally found out the reason why he cheated on my mom, that it was because he wasn't happy, it made me furious! What made me even more furious is that he said if he could go back and make a different decision, he would end up making the same decision because he truly wasn't happy. It felt like my heart was broken all over again. I was beyond angry that night. But, I am still called to forgive him again and again. (Matthew 18:21-22).

When I was at our annual men's retreat with my church during April of 2018, the speaker talked about fathers. God did a healing in my heart during that retreat, where I could finally say that after 16 years of my parents being divorced and after 7 years of walking with Jesus, I was able to not only forgive my dad, but also love my dad. If my heart were a cup, then I felt like all the residue within my heart was completely wiped clean. I was at total peace with my dad. That Sunday of April 22nd, I came home from the men's retreat after experiencing that complete healing and my wife surprised me with something. She had me open up a little shoe box and I found out that day that she was pregnant; I was officially a father! God wiped my heart clean and gave me a new and better promise. God has so much more in store for you and your life, but in order to receive it, you have to forgive.

2 Corinthians 2:10-11 says, "*Now whom you forgive anything, I also forgive. For if indeed I have forgiven anything, I have forgiven that one for your sakes in the presence of Christ, **lest Satan should take advantage of us; for we are not ignorant of his devices.**" Did you catch that? If there is un-forgiveness in your heart then the enemy will take advantage of you. That unforgiveness will fester, grow, and do more damage to you than it will to the offender that you are called to forgive. I felt the call of God in my life when I was 13 years old. He was calling me to come to Him, but the unforgiveness, abandonment, bitterness and anger in my heart led me away from God. I found temporary fulfillment and satisfaction in things that did not really satisfy in the end. The enemy knew my hurt and played on my weakness. But God is so much greater!

**Through His forgiveness towards me, He gave me the power to forgive the one that**

33

*hurt me the most.*

Receive God's forgiveness today, and then give that same Godly forgiveness to someone else. I know they don't deserve it, but neither did we. Is there someone in your past or even present that you need to forgive? God will give you the power to do so if you will ask Him to help you.

## *The second weapon of our warfare is forgiveness!*

# WEAPON THREE
## OUR TESTIMONY

* * *

"I am finally out of here!" I exclaimed, as I was on a plane and on my way to southern California. I decided to make an effort to play football at a junior college in Costa Mesa, California. I just graduated high school and could not wait to get out of my old lifestyle. I wanted to get away from the unhealthy relationship I was in, wanted away from the drug scene, and didn't want to be surrounded by haunting memories of where I grew up in Hillsboro, Oregon. I was finally free! Or so I thought.

In a matter of two weeks, I was back in Hillsboro, Oregon. I did not take into consideration the cost of living in southern California, especially Costa Mesa of all places. My oldest brother lived there, so I thought I could play football and be around family. Monetarily and emotionally, it ended up being too much for a teenager who just graduated high school. My dreams to play college football did not come true. I was immediately submerged into my same old lifestyle back in Hillsboro, Oregon. I quit my job before I left and the position was taken when I got home. I got involved again into the unhealthy relationship with my ex girlfriend, and continued even harder with the drug use. I was devastated. I had no hope. I didn't have a plan B. I was lost, so I did the only thing that I knew to do in that moment. I prayed. I was walking to a job interview at Target and was hoping to God there was more to my life than how I was simply living. I asked God to help me change my life. He heard me! Now this is the starting point of my story.

Revelation 12:11 says, "*And they overcame him (the enemy) by the blood of the Lamb **and by the word of their testimony**, and they did not love their lives to the death.*" The word testimony literally means - evidence. It is vital for us to have evidence of God in our lives. The enemy will present an appealing case before us to prove there is no God, our life is pointless, and there is no hope and no way out. Unless we have evidence to prove him wrong, we will succumb to the enemy's schemes and believe the lies he constantly throws our way.

One thing I have learned in this Christ walk is the enemy never stops harassing us. He floods us daily with thoughts, threats, accusations, and lies (Revelation 12:10). The enemy doesn't play fair. But, we know the great exchange that God has done in our lives, by taking our junk and giving us a brand new start! If we remember that, we can be victorious because of what God has done in our lives. We need to know where we came from in order to know where we are going to.

\* \* \*

*"Then he showed me Joshua the high priest standing before the Angel of the Lord, and* **Satan standing at his right hand to oppose him***. And the Lord said to Satan, "The Lord rebuke you, Satan! The Lord who has chosen Jerusalem rebuke you! Is this not a brand plucked from the fire?"* **Now Joshua was clothed with filthy garments, and was standing before the Angel.** *Then He answered and spoke to those who stood before Him, saying,* **"Take away the filthy garments from him."** *And to him He said,* **"See, I have removed your iniquity from you, and I will**

*clothe you with rich robes." And I said,
"Let them put a clean turban on his head."
So they put a clean turban on his head, and
they put the clothes on him. And the Angel of
the Lord stood by."*

- Zechariah 3:1-5

You have evidence of God working in your life. My prayer is that this story will inspire you to write and know your own, so that you may overcome the power of the enemy by the power of your testimony!

Now, I could start all the way back to when I was a child and talk about all the times that God interceded for me. I will simply put it this way: I felt God working in my life from the moment I had knowledge of my existence. But, I wasn't fully aware of His presence in my life until I was 19 years old and my plans failed. There had to be more to life than drugs, girls, school and work. This desire for more; this freedom is what sparked this testimony in me.

I was just finishing my first year of school at Portland Community College. I began looking for another job. I wasn't playing sports, had a different girlfriend, and was still using drugs. There was a strip of stores near where I lived. Target, Best Buy, Sports Authority, Old Navy, Famous Footwear, and Bed Bath and Beyond. I nearly applied to all of these places the year prior, but never got hired. I decided to go survey the land again and there seemed to be a glow of light surrounding Famous Footwear. I did not apply there before, so I thought I would give it a try. I walked in and talked to the assistant manager. He told me that they were having a group interview later that day. He said he would put a good word in for me if I submitted my application online and showed up to the interview. I did just that. There were about 40 people applying to 4 different locations. The managers asked us why we wanted to work at Famous Footwear and how we could be an asset to the business. People stood up and fired off well crafted responses. Then this one girl stood up and said that she wanted to work at Famous Footwear because she heard that employees get a discount. She said she was just being honest. Then I thought, "and honestly, you are not going to get hired."

I ended up getting the job. But I didn't realize that it was for a bigger and greater purpose than I could ever imagine. I am hesitant to talk too much about myself and tell this long story of mine. But I want us to see that God has been trying to get our attention from the day we were born. He has never left us, He has never forsaken us, He will always be with us. Yes I needed money as a college student, but God knew that I needed so much more than that. I needed Him! He highlighted Famous Footwear for me. He allowed me to get hired on that day out of 40 people. He had two other Christians stationed at Famous Footwear. God was ready to speak to me through them. Esther, who was this 15 year old preacher's daughter, and Baylin, who was this 19 year old Bible College student. For the year I worked there, God spoke to me through them. They prayed for me, encouraged me, had their churches pray for me. Even though I pestered Baylin and gave him a hard time about his faith, he always stood strong. He even called me out one day and quoted a Bible verse to me. I talked about how I believed in God, but my life did not represent Jesus at all. So Baylin said to me, "My dad has this Bible verse written on a 3 x 5 card at home. It says, "Why do you call Me Lord, Lord, and not do the things which I say?" I never felt so upset, and yet so convicted in my life.

Then Esther told me about a preview at Mult-nomah Bible College that was on February 3-4,

2011. This preview allows students to go and stay in the dorms, sit in on classes, and get to know life as a student. It allows you to preview the school before you apply. Why is this significant to my story? After completing 1 year of community college, I had to think about where I would transfer to. I wanted a 4 year degree so I chose to go to Oregon State and major in health. This wasn't my dream, but it was a plan that my girlfriend had, so I decided to join her. My mom asked me if I would consider going to a Christian college. "I didn't know such a place existed." I replied back, "If they had a men's football team I would consider it." A few weeks after that statement, my mom found Multnomah Bible College in Portland. They didn't have a football team, but they did have a basketball team. This caught my attention and I went to the preview.

I was familiar with Christianity and I did believe in God, but I never made the personal decision to follow Jesus. As I attended the chapels, listened to the speakers, watched students raise their hands while they sang to an invisible God, it all became too much for me. The first night in the dorm room I was already calling my girlfriend, who God was telling me I had to leave to follow Him, and was complaining about the preview. Immediately I heard who I now know is the Holy Spirit say to me, "You are not even giving Me a chance!" The next morning I went off campus to smoke a cigarette and began telling God I can't do this for Him. I felt God calling me to be a pastor and attend this Bible College. But I also felt him telling me to leave everything and everyone behind. I was afraid. I sat on the curb, smoked my cigarette, and began crying and telling God why I couldn't follow Him. I said, "This isn't me. All this singing, Bible reading, being Christian, this just isn't me. This isn't who I am." Then God replied to me, "Who are you then?" I replied, "I do not know." In my spirit I heard God say, "Then let Me show you."

The preview was over, but I had a free meal ticket. So I went to the cafeteria before I was planning to leave. I got my free meal and sat at a table by myself. There was only one other person in the cafeteria and he was cleaning. Suddenly, a man came over to me and asked if he could sit with me. He was there for the preview as well. We began to talk, I told him my dilemma, and the decision that I had to make. I told him my conflict between going to Oregon State and then going to Multnomah. I knew that if I went to Oregon State then I would continue to live the life that I tried so hard to get

44

out of. But if I went to Multnomah, I knew it would be blessed, but I knew it would be difficult. This is what he told me. He said, "Daniel, whatever decision you make, whether you go to Oregon State or Multnomah, God will love you either way. But, there will be consequences for whatever decision you make." No one ever told me that God would love me regardless if I chose to follow Him or not (Romans 8:38-39). That touched my heart. But the consequences part really got my attention. He prayed with me and as I left the cafeteria, I saw a tiny prayer chapel on campus. I walked in, got down on my knees and gave my life to Jesus! I was never the same since. Desires for cigarettes, drugs, worldly music, sex before marriage, all changed in that moment. I couldn't live the way that I was living anymore. I left everything behind from my old life and picked up the new life that Jesus Christ offered me. I wish I could say that it was easy from this point on, but it actually became more difficult (Matthew 7:13-14).

I enrolled at Multnomah a few months later in August 2011. I stopped living my old life immediately. But I did struggle for the first year and half of my walk with God. I would do great for a few months and then fall back into my old way. It finally got to a point in August 2012 where I just about did everything God initially delivered me from.

I thought my walk with Him was over, but He spoke to me and said, "Daniel, do you want to do this or not?" Implying, do I want to follow Him or not? I replied back, "Yes God, I don't know how." He said, "You have to trust Me." Two weeks later He led me to the church I have been attending for the past 6 years; East River Fellowship in Hillsboro, Oregon. The moment I walked in the doors I said, "God, Your Spirit is here!"

I was baptized, discipled, married, been to Haiti 4 times, Mexico 5 times, a youth pastor for 5 years, a young adult pastor for 4 years, ordained as a pastor 4 years ago, spoke in main service, taught discipleship classes, baptized people, and have been part of watching God change and transform so many lives around me. This brand new life all came because of Jesus. All He asked me to do was to give up my old life.

## WHAT IS YOUR TESTIMONY?

My wife had the complete opposite of mine. Never got into trouble, saved herself before marriage, never used drugs and yet we both ended up serving the same God in the same church. Do you know what the best testimony is? The one who stayed close to God their entire life. Do you know what the other best testimony is? The one who was so far away from God, but is now close to Him. No matter what your story is, you have a story to tell.

### APPLICATION

Make sure to write out your life before you met Jesus, what happened when you met Him, and what your life looks like after. Be sure to hold onto your story so the enemy can't sway you away from God. Make sure to tell your story to others. You never know who might need to hear it.

## *The third weapon of our warfare is our testimony!*

# WEAPON FOUR
## THE WORD OF GOD

* * *

*"And take the helmet of salvation, **and
the sword of the Spirit, which is
the word of God"***

- Ephesians 6:17

When I was a child, there were two things that I desired to do when I grew up. I wanted to help people and wanted to be a father. I accepted God's calling on my life to be a pastor, and by His grace we have helped a lot of people. All I had to do now was wait patiently for the second desire of my heart to be fulfilled. You have read part of my story already, but I want to stress the importance of this story I am about to share with you, with a little more background of my life. You know that my dad spent eight years in prison, so we had an interesting relationship. He wasn't able to be there for me as we would have liked him to be. I am also one of six children. I have 2 sisters and 3 brothers. One of those brothers is my fraternal twin. My oldest sister has 3 kids: 2 girls and a boy. Her oldest daughter has two kids of her own. My oldest brother has 2 kids: one daughter and one son. My other sister has nine kids: 6 girls and 3 boys. Two of her girls are fraternal twins as well, and one of the twins recently had a son. My older brother has three kids: all boys. My twin brother has 4 kids: two girls and a boy. He also has one girl on the way. I was the only one out of my brothers and sisters who did not have any kids yet. I am currently 28 years old and have been married to my wife for 2 ½ years. That means my mom currently has 21 grandchildren and 3 great grandchildren. Totaling 24 grandkids. You could only imagine the pressure I began to feel as my little nieces even began to have children before me.

But all of that changed on April 22nd, 2018 as my wife surprised me after I got home from our church's men's retreat. As I briefly explained in chapter 2, she put a onesie and the positive pregnancy test in a shoe box and had me open it. As soon as I opened the box I cried immediately. "I knew it!" I shouted. "God told me we were pregnant!" I exclaimed. I was yelling and jumping around that it scared my wife. My oldest sister even gave us the idea to wait to find out the gender of the baby until the day of delivery. My wife's due date was December 22nd, 2018. We were up for the challenge! I remember going to get our first ultrasound done to see how far along she was. The doctor said that they were going to check for two things. They were going to make sure that the baby was growing in the uterus, and they were going to make sure there was a heartbeat. I asked myself, "Why would there not be a heartbeat?" A moment of anxiousness came over me, but suddenly I saw the flashing heart beat on the monitor. Peace came as we looked upon our little baby that literally looked like a gummy bear. It's little nubs for legs and feet were just developing. My wife was eight weeks pregnant.

Since I am a pastor at my church, we were able to announce our exciting news to our entire church congregation. Since my wife and I met at our church we have announced many events of our lives to the church congregation. Like the time we got engaged. We couldn't wait to share our little one with our church family. I will admit that the words of the doctor, "We are going to check if there is a heartbeat" began to haunt me. A spirit of fear came over me, but a brother in Christ was able to identify it, pray for me, and give me a word of encouragement that took that spirit of fear away. Even before we got pregnant, members in our church prophesied about our time of pregnancy. They were spot on with the time and season of the pregnancy. Many prayers and words of encouragement came our way during the time of the pregnancy and we accepted them in faith. It then came time for our 20 week anatomy scan of the baby. Our little one was so active during the ultrasound. Our baby kept turning its back on the doctor, putting their arms over their face to hide, and also swiping their hand to tell us to back off. They knew we were invading their space. I keep saying they because we didn't know their gender and were waiting to find out. The doctors noted that our baby was very active for only 20 weeks. The week prior I felt them kick for the first time. I had my hand on my wife's stomach and she said, "Kick for daddy," and they threw all their might into her belly and I felt it on my hand. We couldn't wait to see our little one.

But then the week of labor day, something didn't seem right. My wife wasn't feeling a lot of movement from our very active baby. We went into the hospital on September 7th to make sure every-thing was alright. The very unexpected and horri-fying scene came on the monitor and the baby was dead. The last time I saw them on the monitor they were moving all around; they had life in them. To see their lifeless body on the monitor this time was a memory I will never forget.

We went home and had an appointment set up the following morning to have my wife induced for labor. She would still have to give birth to our baby who was 6 months old in the womb. I went into our garage, kicked stuff, punched stuff, let out a warrior yell and cried my heart out. We prayed and worshiped all night. Hoping for a miracle. I fell asleep with my hand on her stomach, hoping to feel that kick just one more time. I woke up to the tears of my wife sitting in the baby room afraid of what to do next. We didn't want to go into the hospital, but we knew we had to. As we gained our composure, we went into the hospital to get the second confirmation that our baby was dead. They induced my wife by medication and about 10 hours later my wife gave a still birth to a 1lb 2oz and 12 inch long baby boy. I never cried so hard in my life. He was developed enough to see the features of myself and wife in him. He was 3 months away from being full term. The rest of the experience that Saturday night is too personal to share. But the following morning as the sun began to shine into our hospital room window, I had to gently tell my wife that it was time to let our boy go. The nurse took him into the other room and we made preparations with the local funeral home to prepare the services for him.

We checked out of the hospital Sunday morning and came home to a cold home. I walked in the house with a memory box in my arms instead of with my son. I placed his memory box on the changing table that I set up for him a few weeks prior. I broke down. Friday night, the eerie chill of death was in the air. Saturday night, the pain of loss was so strong that I was cut to my spirit. Sunday morning, was the moment I realized that it would be a little bit longer until I would bring a child into our home. That weekend was one of the toughest moments that I have ever experienced in my young life.

What do you do with that? After everything I explained prior about the relationship with my father. The desire I had to be a father when I got older. I was the only one in my immediate family without children. I am a pastor who is called by

God. The words and prophecies that were spoken over me by my church family. The biggest fear I had, that my baby's heart would stop, finally came true. What do you do with that?

A few weeks after this tragedy, I felt God calling me to read His Word (The Bible). I was not motivated to do this because of the difficult stories in the Bible that I was currently reading through. I was currently reading 1 & 2 Samuel. Death became more noticeable to me. As these biblical stories talked about wars, deception, raids, envy, jealousy, death of men, women, children and even women with children being ripped open. My heart couldn't bear it. I was now more sensitive to death and depravity than I ever have been.

As I felt the stirring in my spirit to read The Bible, I had to be honest before God. I told Him this: "God, I don't want to read your Bible right now. These stories in here are horrible. All the wars, death, destruction, and the fallen state of man are too difficult for me to read. I do not understand why these stories are in here. I do not understand what the point of reading these stories are for. I don't want to read this." But then I went on to say: "I know that you did not give me Your Bible so that I could tell you what I like and don't like about it.

You gave me Your Word in order to tell me who You are and who I am. It doesn't matter if I like Your stories or not. It doesn't matter if I agree with these stories or not. You gave Your Word to me to show me the truth. But I can't discern Your Word on my own. I need Your help Holy Spirit. Please help me understand what You are trying to say through Your Word. Amen."

Then I opened up my Bible and the next chapter of Scripture for me to read was 2 Samuel 11. **Please take a moment to read it.**

This was not encouraging at all. It seemed to make matters worse and to solidify the hardship in my heart. At the end of verse 27 it says, "*But the thing that David had done displeased the LORD.*" Thank you! Finally some sign of life. Finally there is some type of justice. I couldn't stand to read all the horrors that took place in the Bible and in my life and yet there was nothing done about it. I said to God, "God, You have to show me who You are right now. I never saw you as a God of the Old Testament and then a God of the New Testament. I believe in Jesus and all His goodness, but I am finding it hard to simply throw out the Old Testament books and all the difficult passages of Scripture that are in there. For the first time God, I am struggling to see

You as the same God throughout the entire Bible. You need to show me who You really are in the midst of all this darkness and tragedy. Please show me that You are who You say You are."

I kept reading and I noticed these words in 2 Samuel 12:1 - *"Then the LORD sent Nathan to David."* Through all the tragedy of the story in chapter 11 God's response was not one of wrath, but He responded by sending. I knew that names in the Bible had to do with the stories being told. I looked up what Nathan meant and his name literally means "gift from God." The name David means, "beloved." In this passage, God sent a gift on behalf of David. Where else do I see that term gift in the Bible?

Ephesians 2:8-9 says, *"For by grace you have been saved through faith, and that not of yourselves; it is **the gift of God**, not of works, lest anyone should boast."* This drew my attention to the context of 2 Samuel 12 and I understood it like I never have before. Nathan (the gift from God) shared a story with David that convicted his heart.

David came to this conclusion after his conviction, *"So David said to Nathan, I have sinned against the LORD." **(see Psalm 51)**. And Nathan said to David, "The LORD also has put away your*

57

*sin; you shall not die.*" (Verse 13). The gift from God took the place of David's sin. David received this gift as he recognized and admitted his sin. Though David didn't die, there were consequences to follow. Immediate consequences (his first born son from Bathsheba would die). Later consequences (strife within his family).

The story continues, *"David therefore pleaded with God for the child, and David fasted and went in and lay all night on the ground."* This is a picture of David's old nature dying. The child died and this is how David responds. *"So David arose from the ground, washed and anointed himself, and changed his clothes; and he went into the house of the LORD and worshipped"* (Verse 20). Is this not a picture of the new life God has given us?

David then breaks his fast and makes this statement: *"But now he is dead; why should I fast? Can I bring him back again? I shall go to him, but he shall not return to me."* (Verse 23). The story goes on to say that David and Bathsheba had a son named Solomon and that the LORD loved him. The name Solomon means "peace." This made me think of Romans 5:1, *"Therefore, having been justified by faith, **we have peace with God** through our Lord Jesus Christ."*

What the Holy Spirit showed me in this chapter of Scripture was the Gospel. In the midst of all the tragedy, hurt, pain, deceit, selfishness, adultery, death, murder, cowardness, lying, backbiting, and all the other downfalls of human nature, God is present! The hurt in my heart made me cry to God and ask Him to do something about this heartache and tragedy in my life. I asked Him to give me some sign of hope in the midst of this struggle. As I read this difficult passage in the Bible it was as if a hologram of Jesus popped from the page and I felt God say to me, "I did do something about it. I gave My Son." In the midst of it all, in the midst of this crazy thing we call life, God is present and He has provided a hope!

Two days prior to this revelation, God gave me a vision during our youth service. I saw Jesus standing in our youth room. As everyone was raising their hands, He was standing and smiling. Then He asked me what I wanted. I paused for a moment and responded, "I need hope." Then my emotions came rushing in and within my heart I began to struggle. I told Him that I need hope now and I feel like He isn't giving me what I need; it seems out of my grasp. Immediately Jesus said, "You are looking at Him." (Colossians 1:27).

I will never know the full answer as to why my son's heart stopped in the womb. So much came against my wife and son that year. But they made it through every trial. He was a strong boy. I am proud of his mom for carrying him that far. I am proud of them both, for not giving up. The doctors offered to do an autopsy on him, but I declined. Even though I will never know what happened to my son, I know that I will see him again. I believe that I will spend eternity in heaven with my boy (Revelation 21-22). All I can do is trust God.

We named him Joseph Lael Aguilar. Joseph is my middle name, but it is also prophetic. Joseph means that God will add and give increase. I named my son Joseph to declare that God will provide my wife and I with other children. Joseph is also significant because he went ahead of his family into Egypt. Even though the biblical Joseph went through so many trials, his sacrifice paved the way to save his family. Lael means belongs to God. He belonged to God before he ever belonged to me. I will never forget my boy and he will forever be engraved on the tablet of my heart. I can't wait for the day when I can see him again. But I know that the time is not yet.

How does this tragic story play into spiritual

warfare? How does this tragedy have anything to do with the enemy? I am glad you asked. I am reminded of Luke 22:31-34:

*"And the Lord said, "Simon, Simon! Indeed,* **Satan has asked for you, that he may sift you as wheat.** *But I have prayed for you, that* **your faith should not fail;** *and* **when you have returned to Me,** *strengthen your brethren."*
*But he said to Him, "Lord, I am ready to go with You, both to prison and to death." Then He said, "I tell you, Peter, the rooster shall not crow this day before you will deny three times that you know Me."*

The enemy is always looking for an opportunity to shake our faith. In the midst of trials, the enemy wants us to question the character of God (Job 1-2). Whether it be hardships, failures, sin, etc. Difficult times create ample opportunity for the enemy to move in on us (1 Peter 5:8-9).

But Jesus prays that Peter's faith will not fail him.

So where do we get faith? Romans 10:17 - *"So then faith comes by hearing, and hearing by*

*the word of God."* We need faith in God to endure trials. Faith in His character. Faith, that He is
who He says He is. God tells us who He is through
His Word. As I stated above from 2 Samuel 12, "God
is present in the midst of our circumstances." That
truth helped me to stand firm in the midst of great
adversity. It is important that you have God's Word
firmly planted in your heart (Mark 4). The enemy
will strike more than once on the same issue. But
our game plan doesn't change. We stop him with
God's Word!

Only because of God's truth am I able to
stand. Getting into His Word is the only way to
build a solid life in Jesus. I have many examples of
how God has spoken through His Word to me and
built me up. But this is one example that I will never
forget.

APPLICATION

Have you been through a hardship that made
you question God's character? Is your current
thought life at odds ends with God? I encourage
you to get in His Word! Pray and ask God where
you should start reading in the Bible. Before you
start reading, ask the Holy Spirit to help you dis-

cern what God is wanting to tell you. Once Holy Spirit reveals the truth to you, then match it up to the lie of the enemy. His truth will defeat the lie!

### *The fourth weapon of our warfare is the Word of God!*

# WEAPON FIVE
## LOVE

* * *

The first time I walked into my church East River Fellowship, I said, "God, Your Spirit is here!" That is the entire reason I stayed, because the Spirit gives life and He alone does the transforming work that we need (John 6:63). But I noticed that something else was there when I walked in the church. A girl dressed beautifully and worshipping God beautifully as the song leader sang. I thought, "this is my kind of church!" I sat behind her two different times and introduced myself. Her name is Sonja who is now my wife. We got to know each other more as we went on our first missions trip to Haiti together. We were on this trip for 17 days with waves of missionaries coming and going. But, we stayed with each other for the entire 17 days. I saw her heart on this trip. She held the sick children, ate the food set before her without complaining, shared her Bible reading journals so humbly and passionately and boy could she dance! Haitians have rhythm, but Sonja had rhythm that even made the Haitians jealous.

The moment I knew that Sonja was different from any other girls is when she asked me the million dollar question. "So, what made you want to be a pastor?" A few others sat around us and I began my vocal journal. People got up and walked away, not amused or interested in my story anymore. But Sonja sat with me the entire time and listened. I thought my response was 20 minutes, she said it was an hour or more. But she stayed by my side. The next morning, I was walking from one side of the orphanage to the other and as I looked at the front porch I saw her interacting with the kids as she normally did and I knew that I loved her. But there was so much junk in my heart that it kept me from her.

As we got back from our trip, Sonja began helping me serve in the youth ministry. I was the brand new youth pastor. I also started my senior year at Multnomah Bible College. A lot was thrown at me that year and in the years to come. I went on a three year faith battle that not only tested my faith, but almost wrecked it. My view of God was challenged by both conservative and charismatic Christians. I couldn't seem to hear his voice clearly during that season. This made it difficult for me to know who was right and what was right. I had no clue what I was doing in the youth ministry; trying to serve the teenagers and lead the adults. And the worst part about it is that I began to resort back to characteristics from my past life. I was walking with Jesus for about 3 years at this point.

Because I was acting like my old self, I began to treat Sonja like my old self would. I had a temptation to call my ex-girlfriend who I haven't talked to in years. God told me not to do it, but I did anyway. There was no answer. I told Sonja about my battle with this, but I did not tell her that I made the phone call. Sonja and I ended up dating in April 2014. I made that phone call to my ex a few weeks after Sonja and I began to date. When my birthday and holidays came around, Sonja would go above and beyond for me. She would buy me gifts or make me gifts. She would get my favorite food or dessert. She worked at Starbucks and would bring me pound bags of coffee. She poured her heart out into the youth and never asked for anything in return. She even got me things like car fresheners because I had an old car that the teenage boys would stink up because they didn't know how to properly apply deodorant. Other guys tried dating her, but she respectfully turned them away. Sonja saved her purity until her wedding day. She was waiting for her husband and believed that it was me. But I did not reciprocate the same devotion and love back to her. The love and devotion that she rightfully deserved.

We would hang out late, but I never drove her home or picked her up. I wouldn't even follow her home in my car as she drove herself to the other side of town to see me. I was still talking to other girls while we were courting and I made that foolish phone call after we were dating. I never gave her gifts or cards. When she was struggling with family issues, I didn't hold her and respond appropriately. We even went on a date to Burgerville and I purchased the meal. It was not cheap for a poor college student. We sat down and she wanted barbecue sauce. I didn't realize how much my wife loves barbecue sauce. She asked if she could get some and my reply was, "Only if they don't charge you extra." The server felt so bad for Sonja that she just gave her the barbecue sauce. What was wrong with me? I pushed her away and never gave her all of my heart. I couldn't give what I didn't have.

I didn't have love in my heart, so I couldn't give it back.

One day she began telling me about how much she appreciates me. She said she was so thankful that even though we have been through a lot of emotional ups and downs, we have made it this far in our relationship. She forgave me for all the little things I didn't do right. She knew I had to learn how to treat a girl right. She knew my past lifestyle. She said the one thing that really gave her hope was that I didn't call my ex-girlfriend. All the other things I did wrong didn't matter, but not making that one phone call kept her heart full. So I confessed and told her that I made the call months ago. When she found out that it was after we started dating, she was heartbroken. My decision told Sonja she wasn't enough for me. She was ready to give all of herself to me in marriage, but that decision showed her I wasn't satisfied with her. I told her she should leave. But then I responded, "You are all I have left." There was no excuse for my poor decision, but I had a lot of junk in my heart. It was coming out and it was affecting my relationships. Especially the relationship with my future wife.

We made it to our one year dating anniversary and she made me a gift. It was a giant mason jar with many multicolored pieces of paper in it. When I asked her what it was, she replied, "It's 365 reasons why I love you." As God as my witness, every reason was different. How could she find 365 reasons to love me? Especially after the way I had treated her for the past 1 and a half years? The foundational verse for this act of love came from Proverbs 10:12 - **love covers all sins**.

I had been in relationships prior where cheating and lying were part of the norm. That's just what you did in a relationship. In my previous relationship prior to my wife, the person let me do anything and was okay with it. They didn't care what I did, as long as I was happy. That's not love. Love isn't letting people do whatever they want. Love is closely related to mercy. This means you give people what they don't deserve. You love them unconditionally, regardless of what they do to you. Now, this is going to look different towards certain people. Ask God for discernment on how to love that person. Ask when or if you should be around them. I will leave that decision between you and the Lord.

I first experienced unconditional love from God who died and forgave me for all my sins (Romans 5:8). But I also needed to experience love through His daughter (Sonja) made in His image. I figured God would love me because He is perfect and is big enough. But I didn't think Sonja would be bold enough to call me out on my stuff and yet still love me with all her heart. We ended up getting married on March 5, 2016. God has worked through this woman to change me! She has never stopped loving me and she still encourages me to be a better man and husband everyday.

## WHAT'S THE POINT OF ALL THIS?

Love destroys darkness! The entire Gospel is motivated by love. John 3:16, 1 John 4, Ephesians 1, Romans 5:8 all prove that God did what He did out of love. We all need a Sonja in our lives. Someone to always be by our side and love us no matter what. Someone who doesn't let us do whatever we want, but loves us no matter what we do. Receiving the love of God and the love from my wife removed darkness from my heart. I had a lot of fear, depression, anxiousness, hurt, pain, regret and selfishness. 1 John 4:18 says, *"There is no fear in love; but perfect love casts out fear, because fear involves torment. But he who fears has not been made perfect in love."* God brought Sonja into my life to drive out the fear!

I received God's infinite love the moment I gave my life to Jesus. But I had to learn how to be loved and how to give that love back. I received God's supernatural love, but He was going to prove His tangible love, not just through the cross, but through my wife. Love doesn't only have to come through a wife. This unconditional love can also be through a friend, coworker, family member, or even a stranger. Whoever it comes through, it needs to be received and reciprocated.

## WHY DOES IT MATTER?

Because Jesus said in John 13:34-35, *"A new commandment I give to you, that you love one another; as I have loved you, that you also love one another. By this all will know that you are My disciples, if you have love for one another."* Jesus also says in John 17 that the world will know that Father God sent Him if we allow God's love to flow through us and we love each other.

\* \* \*

## APPLICATION

Who have you been pushing away? Who is trying to show you love, but you keep refusing? Is it God Himself? Who is in your life that needs God's love? Are you willing to give it to them?

First, we must receive God's love. Don't refuse it. His love will transform you. Then go out and show that same love to the world.

### *The fifth weapon of our warfare is love!*

# WEAPON SIX
## PRAYER

*  *  *

I remember being six years old and having a 104 degree fever. My mom was a Christian for about 11 years at this point. We did not have medical insurance and over the counter medicine was not helping me. My mom would put an ice cold towel on my head and within seconds it would turn lukewarm. My mom was praying the entire time for a miracle. After many failed attempts to control my fever, fear entered my mom. "I am taking you to the doctor!" she exclaimed, and rushed out of the bedroom door. I was laying down on the bed and was facing the bedroom wall. The light in the room was turned off because I had such a bad headache. She shut the door on her way out which made the room completely dark.

Within a few seconds the room lit up with light. I had my eyes halfway open because of my headache, but there was an obvious light in the room and I said, "Mom please turn the light off." She didn't answer. Again I said, "Mom, please turn the light off." Again, no answer. I thought she came into the room, but I wasn't sure why she wasn't answering. So I began to say again, "Mom, turn the light off," and as I turned to look towards the door, I saw the brightest light I have ever seen. A figure of a man was standing behind my door and the beam of the light coming from him and that room corner was brilliant! The light was so bright that I could not see his face. But, I did see the white gown at his feet and the appearance of a body. So I screamed and my mom barged into the room. As she opened the door, the light in the room went out and the light from the hallway shone in. My mom turned the room light on and checked my temperature to see if my fever was rising. The beep signaled and my temperature was at 98.6 degrees. I was completely healed!

Matthew 8:14-15 says, *"Now when Jesus had come into Peter's house, He saw his wife's mother lying sick with a fever. So He touched her hand, and the fever left her. And she arose and served them."*

Acts 12:7 says, *"Now behold, an angel of the Lord stood by him, and a light shone in the prison;*

*and he struck Peter on the side and raised him up, saying, "Arise quickly!" And his chains fell off his hands."*

The point of this chapter is not meant to talk about Divine healing or the ministry of angels. However I do believe in both for today. This chapter is meant to address the need for prayer. God is sovereign and all knowing. Nonetheless, the Bible commands us to pray (1 Thessalonians 4:17). Ephesians 6 is often referenced when discussing the topic of spiritual warfare. After enlisting the armor of God, the apostle Paul says this, ***"praying always with all prayer and supplication in the Spirit**, being watchful to this end with all perseverance and supplication for all the saints"* (verse 18). A vital weapon in spiritual war is prayer! Notice what verse 17 of Ephesians 6 references before he mentions prayer; *"the sword of the Spirit, which is **the word of God."*** We need to stand on the foundation of the Word, if we want to pray effectively in the spirit!

Prayer means to make a request, to appeal, to declare, to speak out, to communicate, etc. As one of our youth students put it plainly, "Prayer is talking with God." It is all about having a relationship with God. He wants us to pray so we can

77

have fellowship with Him. Jesus would sneak away often to pray to His Father. I believe He received His next marching orders. But I also believe Jesus wanted and needed to spend time with His Father. If Jesus snuck away to pray, then shouldn't we? In times of prayer, we are called to declare things and set situations in order through the power, authority, and the Name of Jesus Christ. We are called to pray heavenly circumstances into reality (Psalm 119:89). Nothing in the physical will change, until it is addressed in the spiritual. This comes through the power of prayer! (See Daniel 9-11).

Other times of prayer consists of us simply slowing down and spending time with our Heavenly Father. This helps us realign ourselves with His will for our lives. Before we begin to declare and rebuke darkness, we need to understand the foundational characteristics of prayer. I have to make the same request the disciples made of Jesus.

### TEACH ME HOW TO PRAY

*"In this manner, therefore, pray: Our Father in heaven, Hallowed be Your name."*
- Matthew 6:8-9

It is difficult to pray when you don't know who you are praying to.

First we need to understand that our Heavenly Father is distinct from all other father figures. A man was telling me that he was terrified when he found out that his wife was pregnant. Not because he didn't love his wife or didn't want children. He was afraid because he knew that he would have the responsibility of representing Father God to his child. Imitating God is a huge role to fill. But regardless of mistakes that man has made in the name of God, we can trust the character of our Heavenly Father.

There was this season in my life where I felt the overwhelming urge to share the gospel with as many people as possible. I was looking for opportunities to manifest the gifts of the Holy Spirit and bring people into relationship with God. I know that is the work of the Holy Spirit, and I was eager to work with Him. Though I was bold and had some successes, I also had a lot of failures. One day I let fear creep into my heart and I did not talk to someone that I felt strongly led to talk to about Jesus. I was driving in my work van and began to cry. I spouted off all my mistakes and told God that I can't seem to get this Christian lifestyle down properly.

Then a surprising sentence came out of my mouth and I said, "Please don't leave me!" Immediately I heard God say, "You have not been abandoned, you have been adopted!" The Scripture the Holy Spirit referenced was from Romans 8:15-16, *"For you did not receive the spirit of bondage again to fear, but you received the Spirit of adoption by whom we cry out, 'Abba, Father.' The Spirit Himself bears witness with our spirit that we are children of God."*

God showed me that when my dad left my mom, I thought he left me. I thought I wasn't good enough for my earthly father, which made me believe I wasn't enough for my Heavenly Father. God assured me that I was more than enough and that He would never leave me (Deuteronomy 31:8). He gave me another chance to minister to someone that very day and that's exactly what I did.

It is difficult to pray when you don't know who you are praying to. We need to remember that we are praying to a good Heavenly Father that can't be negatively compared to our earthly father. This accurate knowledge of Father God helps me approach him in prayer.

*"Your kingdom come. Your will be done on*

*earth as it is in heaven. Give us this day our*
*daily bread."*

- Matthew 6:10-11

It is difficult to pray when you don't know what to ask for.

This part of Scripture tells us to pray Heaven down to earth daily. But what is in Heaven and can I really ask for it?

We just had a garage sale at our house. We had an entire box full of walkie talkies and the chargers to go with it. The neighbor boy came over and bought two walkie talkies and a charger for $3. The next day he comes back and says that one of the walkie talkies doesn't work. So he asked for an exchange. I had a bunch of these walkie talkies so I exchanged the broken one for a new one and also gave him two more for free. A few hours later he comes back and asks for another charging station. He said, "Since you gave me two more walkie talkies, I now have four but with only one charger. I need another charger!" He didn't offer to pay, nor did he shy away from asking. Do you know why? Because he saw how many walkie talkies and chargers I had, so it only makes sense to give him another charging port. Especially since I gave him two walkie talkies for free! If he comes back and asks for the entire bag, then I will give it all to him no problem.

God is asking us to look into Heaven and see all that He has available for us (Colossians 3:1). He is pleading with us to ask for whatever it is that we need (Matthew 7:7-8). The reason why we don't receive is because we don't ask (James 4:2b). Joy, peace, friendship, love, marriage, finances, life calling, wisdom, guidance, strength, safety, protection, salvation, health, justice, etc. is all made available to us! We simply need to know what is available and then have the confidence to ask for it! (1 John 5:14).

*"And forgive us our debts, as we forgive our debtors."*

\- Matthew 6:12

It is difficult to pray when you don't know who you are.

During my first season of basketball at Multnomah Bible College, we ended our first semester against a difficult opponent. It was the last game until our winter break in 2011. If we won this game it would be our 10th win, and this would qualify us to go to a tournament in Joplin, Missouri in the spring of 2012. Coach really wanted this win. At the beginning of the school year, coach set out a list of ground rules. He was not only concerned about our basketball record, he was concerned about our record of life. He wanted to teach us character, so he put rules in place in order to shape us. They were simple rules such as: go to class on time, don't skip class, turn in all assignments, no texting during class, sit in the front row of class, etc. Everyone did good at the start of the year.

A few days before our final game of the semester, coach decided to check in on how we were doing with these rules he set for us. He stood in front of the white board in the locker room and asked us to be honest if we did not meet one or more of these requirements. He told us to go up to the white board and write on it what we failed to accomplish. One by one we all went up and put down what we failed to do. The white board was covered with mistakes we had made. Coach was not very pleased. In order to teach us our lesson, he planned for us to come in early the morning before our winter break to have practice without basketballs. This meant that we would run all morning long. I was a commuter and lived an hour away with traffic. I was not looking forward to that practice.

It ended up being half time during this difficult game and we were losing. Coach was furious about our playing style on and off the court at this point. As he paced around the locker room to find some sort of motivation for the team, he saw the white board with all of our mistakes written on it. He looked at us and said, "If you win, then you won't have to run tomorrow morning." He said, "If you go out and beat this team, then I will let you off the hook!" Our eyes widened and our hearts lit up with joy. We walked out of that locker room and played as if we all partook of "Michael Jordan's secret stuff" from Space Jam! We won the game in triple over time!

We ran back in the locker room celebrating, shouting, dancing and singing. Then one of our players looked at the white board and wiped his arms across all the mistakes we had made. This blotted out all of them! It was certainly a night to remember.

Colossians 2:13-14 says, *"And you, being dead in your trespasses and the uncircumcision of your flesh, He has made alive together with Him, having **forgiven you all trespasses, having wiped out the handwriting of requirements that was***

**against us,** *which was contrary to us. And* **He has taken it out of the way,** *having* **nailed it to the cross."**

Too often we feel like my first year basketball team. We feel burdened by our mistakes. We recognize our wrongs and we let it affect the way we play the game of life. But what freed us to play and win, was a hope that our debt would be paid. When it comes to Jesus, we don't have to cross our fingers and hope we are forgiven. It says that we are forgiven...for everything! Knowing who we are frees us up to pray. We are forgiven and covered.

*"And do not lead us into temptation, but deliver us from the evil one. For Yours is the kingdom and the power and the glory forever. Amen."*

- Matthew 6:13

It is difficult to pray when you don't know where you are going.

It is interesting that Jesus tells us not to pray to be led into temptation (or testing, depending on the context of the biblical passage). Because, in Matthew 4:1 it says, *"Then* **Jesus was led up by the Spirit** *into the wilderness* **to be tempted** *by*

85

*the devil."* In Matthew 4:11, that part of the story ends with, ***"Then the devil left Him, and behold, angels came and ministered to Him."*** We know from James 1:13 that God does not tempt anyone. We know from 2 Thessalonians 3:3 that the Lord is faithful and will guard us from the evil one. So what is going on here? What is Jesus trying to tell us about this portion of prayer?

I will never forget the first date I went on with my now wife. Five years ago, Sonja and I went to a frozen yogurt shop in the area. It was October in Hillsboro Oregon; true Oregonians. I had the same feeling of butterflies in my stomach as I did when I played my first football game at 10 years old. We had an amazing time and I thank God that we are now married. But I was also going through a tough transition in my faith journey. I remember telling her this vision that God gave me. He showed me a little kid on a bike. The father was holding the handle bars while the kid rode joyously around the street block. Then he showed me the father letting go of the handlebars and the child began to ride alone. I heard the Spirit speak to me and say, "I am letting go of the handlebars with you." This terrified me.

For the first two and a half years of my walk

with God, I could hear Him audibly. He spoke audibly to me when He said, "You are going to Multnomah and you are going to be a pastor!" (See Acts 13:2). He would continue to speak audibly to me and tell me to not talk to certain people, to go to a certain place to get a job, would highlight Scripture and speak on it immediately, and so many more examples. I remember somebody in our church saying to me, "God clearly speaks to you. I can tell." But right around this time of the "bike riding and letting go of the handlebars vision," I went on my first missions trip. I went to Haiti. This is the same trip where I met my wife. Being there for 15 days and working with orphans, preaching the gospel, encouraging church leaders, and loving the people changed my life.

On the way home from Haiti, we had a connecting flight from Florida to Washington. I sat next to a gentleman and he asked me what I was doing in Florida. I told him all about my trip and how good God is. He then fired back with, "I bet I can guess 9 out of 10 things that you believe about your God and I can counter every one of them!" He called himself a mathematician. For the next 3 hours, this man told me all about why he doesn't believe that God exists. Anything I said he had a rebuttal. I was about to begin my senior year at Multnomah Bible College the day we got back from Haiti. I did not have much to say to him at this point and I simply stood my ground. He then proceeded to tell me the real reason that he doesn't believe in God. He served as an altar boy in his catholic church and he said that he was sexually abused by five different catholic priests. He then asked me, "If there was a perfect and loving God, then why would He let that happen to me?" I told him that God didn't do that to him. We live in a fallen world (Genesis 3-4) and man is capable of doing horrible things.

This was just the beginning of the trials that lay ahead of me. For the next three years, I struggled with my faith. What started off so romantically, very quickly became a nightmare. I could not hear God audibly at all. My Bible college professors would tell me what they believed about God and the Bible, then my church would tell me what they believed about God and the Bible; they were completely opposite views. Issues from my past began to spring up, I was in a new relationship with Sonja, I was the youth pastor at my church and only five months into it. When I needed to hear God most, I couldn't hear Him at all. I received two prophecies that helped encourage me during those trying years. I also had to hold onto what God had already spoken to me; through His Word and audibly by His Spirit.

I remember fasting from food for 24 hours. Right when I got to the end of my spiritual breaking point, I heard in my spirit, "The devil wants you to quit." That was the first time I heard anything from God in what seemed like forever. That was enough for me to know that I had to endure what I was going through. I recognized the source that was trying to end my walk of faith (John 10:10). I also knew that it would be over someday. As Jesus went through the wilderness temptations in Matthew 4, so I had to go through the wilderness as well. One of those prophecies that I spoke of above came to me right after this revelation. It was perfect timing and within a few months, I was out of that desert period. I began to hear God audibly again.

I remember asking God what happened for those three years. Why did I have to go through that? As Jesus walked, so we must walk (1 Peter 2:21). But I remember saying to God, "Please God, don't ever let me go through that again. Whatever it was I didn't like it." Then God replied, "You will never go through that type of situation again. But I can't promise that you won't go through hardship in the future." We know that God tests us (Deuteronomy 8:2, Genesis 22:1). We also know that God will never tempt us (James 1:13). The difference is that with testing, God wants us to prevail. But with tempting the enemy wants us to fail. It was never part of God's original plan to put us through difficult situations. There was no need to. We had everything we needed in the garden of Eden. He simply asked us to choose Him and that we didn't do (Genesis 2-3). We were made in His image (Genesis 1:27), but we have been so distorted from the original image He made us in. Therefore, it is necessary for Him to shape us through trials and tribulations (James 1).

Getting back to Jesus' statement of, "and do not lead us into temptation, but deliver us from the evil one." He is not referring to testing and hardship as we just discussed. We will go through testing and we will go through hardship. He is telling us to pray that God will keep us away from temptation. Praying that we will stay clear of temptation (Proverbs 4:14-15). Temptation does us no good. It's end goal is to lead us to death (James 1:15). God will never lead you into temptation! God is so good, that when we find ourselves in temptation, then He is the one who gets us out of it (1 Corinthians

10:13). So, don't let hardships keep you away from following God. As you pray to God, know that you will encounter hardship. Know that God will never set you up to be overcome by evil. Know that God is ultimately leading your life for good!

## REMEMBER

- Our Heavenly Father is distinct from all other father figures.
- Find out what is in Heaven and pray it down to earth daily.
- Knowing who you are frees you to pray effectively.
- God will lead you ultimately to good.

## APPLICATION

What part of the Lord's prayer do you struggle with the most? What part comes most naturally to you? Start by praying from what you know. Then, seek out Scriptures and Bible studies to help you strengthen the areas that you struggle to pray from. God wants us to be well rounded in our prayer lives!

*"The effective, fervent prayer of a righteous man avails much."*

- James 5:16b

### The sixth weapon of our warfare is prayer!

# WEAPON SEVEN
## THE BLOOD OF JESUS

* * *

*"**And they overcame him by the blood of the Lamb** and by the word of their testimony, and they did not love their lives to the death."*
- Revelation 12:11

One night during an event at my church, I looked at my wife and noticed that she looked more pale than I have ever seen her. We took her into the hospital and they said her blood level had dropped dramatically. She was at a 7.4 blood level and they wanted to do a blood infusion. My first response was "No!" I scheduled an iron transfusion instead. However, my wife felt horrible. She was not able to function with this low level of blood. The doctors were surprised that she was even walking around. Within 24 hours, we had to take her back to the hospital. Her blood level dropped to a 7.2. The doctor asked why she left the hospital in the first place. The doctor continued to tell us that my wife could go into cardiac arrest if she didn't receive a blood infusion. My wife was struggling with some health concerns that was making her lose blood. We had no other choice but to go forward with the blood infusion. They had to put two units of blood in her which brought her blood level up to a 10.4. The new blood saved her life!

Many people are in this same situation today when it comes to faith in God. They are functioning, but are not functioning at the level of life they should be. They are on the verge of spiritual death and yet continue their lives as if nothing is wrong. When it comes time to solve the problem, they refuse The Blood. People try almost anything else to be saved. The problem is, there is no other solution. Just like my wife's case in the physical, only the blood of Jesus can save us and cover us in the spiritual!

## WHY BLOOD?

*"Now the Lord spoke to Moses and Aaron in the land of Egypt, saying, "This month shall be your beginning of months; it shall be the*

first month of the year to you. Speak to all the congregation of Israel, saying: 'On the tenth of this month **every man shall take for himself a lamb**, according to the house of his father, **a lamb for a household**...

**Your lamb shall be without blemish, a male of the first year.** You may take it from the sheep or from the goats. Now you shall keep it until the fourteenth day of the same month. Then the whole assembly of the congregation of Israel **shall kill it** at twilight. And they shall **take some of the blood** and put it on the two doorposts and on the lintel of the houses where they eat it...

Now **the blood shall be a sign for you** on the houses where you are. And **when I see the blood, I will pass over you;** and the plague shall not be on you to destroy you when I strike the land of Egypt."

- Exodus 12:1-13

Based on this passage of Scripture we see:
- The blood could not come from just any source
- The sacrifice had to be a lamb without blemish
- The sacrifice had to be a male
- The lamb had to die

- The blood had to be applied
- The blood became a covering
- When judgment came, the judgment would pass over (not touch) the places with the blood on it.
- Those people would remain alive

## THE LIFE IS IN THE BLOOD

*"For the life of the flesh is in the blood, and I have given it to you upon the altar to make atonement for your souls; for it is the blood that makes atonement for the soul.' ... for it is the life of all flesh. Its blood sustains its life."*

-Leviticus 17:11, 14

Based on this passage of Scripture we see:
- Life is in the blood
- It covers and qualifies our soul
- It sustains our lives

Let's look at Hebrews for even further clarification: Hebrews 9:22, *"And according to the law almost all things are purified with blood, and without shedding of blood there is no remission of sins."*

Hebrews 9:13, *"For if **the blood of bulls and goats** and the ashes of a heifer, sprinkling the unclean, sanctifies for the purifying of the flesh,"*

Hebrews 10:4, *"For it is not possible that the blood of bulls and goats could take away sins."*

## THE PROBLEM

The Jewish people knew they did wrong and needed a covering for their sins. God revealed His law (His will for living) to the Jewish people. They fell short and did not meet these expectations (Romans 3:23). Therefore, they were deemed imperfect. How can someone who is imperfect have relationship with a holy and perfect God? God doesn't want His creation separate from Him, but sin did just that (Isaiah 59:2). Since there was a price that needed to be paid for reconciliation, blood was the price that would pay the debt. The Jewish people would then take the proper animal, place their hands on it and transfer their sins to the animal (Leviticus). They would kill the animal in order to shed it's blood. Once the blood spilled out, the price for sin would be paid and that person would be covered. They would be guiltless. But there still remained a huge problem. Man caused this sin to come into the world (Genesis 3), so man had to pay for it.

But, based on the Scriptures in Hebrews, animal blood was not enough to cover man's sins. The sin of man is a spiritual matter. Therefore it had to be covered in a spiritual way. Animal blood simply would not suffice. Man needed perfect blood from a man in order to cover the sins of man. Animal blood could not take the place of man's blood. Since no man is perfect (Romans 3:10-12), then where could we get perfect human blood from?

## The answer

God is perfect and His ways are perfect (Matthew 5:48, Psalm 18:30). God qualifies to be the perfect sacrifice. But God does not have a physical body (Numbers 23:19), which means He doesn't have any blood. According to John 4 God is Spirit. If only God had a body that His perfect blood could be poured out from...look at Hebrews 10:5-7.

*"Therefore, when He came into the world, He said: "Sacrifice and offering You did not desire, **but a body You have prepared for Me**. In burnt offerings and sacrifices for sin you*

*had no pleasure. Then I said, 'Behold, I have*
*come — In the volume of the book it is writ-*
*ten of Me — To do Your will, O God.'""*

Jesus came down from Heaven and became the perfect sacrifice for us (Philippians 2). Jesus remained sinless (without spot or blemish). Jesus is fully man (physical) and fully God (spiritual). So He not only carries the perfect blood, but He had the body for the blood to pour out from!

The story of Exodus is brought full circle when we read John 1:29 and see what God's heart was from the very beginning. *"The next day John saw Jesus coming toward him and said, "Behold!* **The Lamb of God who takes away the sin of the world!"**

I did an outreach at a local community college earlier this year. I printed off this quote by Mahatma Gandhi, "I like your Christ. I do not like your Christians. Your Christians are so unlike your Christ." This affirms the imperfection and fallen state of mankind, while affirming Jesus' perfection. As I walked around the school, I approached students and said something like this: "I admit that the Church has done horrible acts. I admit that Christians have done terrible acts. But what has Christ done that was so bad?" Students who didn't even believe the Gospel could not answer back with anything else other than, "Jesus has done nothing wrong." At the end of all four Gospels (Matthew, Mark, Luke, John) it talks about Jesus and His crucifixion. Matthew 27:37-38 says this, *"And they put up over His head the accusation written against Him: THIS IS JESUS THE KING OF THE JEWS. Then two robbers were crucified with Him, one on the right and another on the left."*

If I had to hang on that cross, then what would my accusations be? Could you imagine, being stripped nearly naked, nailed to cross, bleeding, suffering, ashamed, embarrassed, mocked and ridiculed. All your friends, family and the entire world looking at you as you are stuck helpless. All the while, you have every sin pinned over your head for the entire world to see. How embarrassed would you be? Jesus was on the cross for six hours! Could you imagine a six hour long movie of your life on display for all to see? This would not be like social media, where people show only the highlights of their lives. The accusations written against you, all the evil ever done, all the sin ever done, all the dark things ever done, would be on display and would describe you for not only those six hours; It would define your legacy and your lineage. Your family would be shamed.

And yet Jesus took all of our sin from us. Jesus took all of our accusations and put it on Himself. Every dark thing has become light. Every secret sin is covered by the Blood of the Lamb. Every single sin that kept us from God The Father, Jesus has taken out of the way and nailed it to the cross! The only accusation that would represent us today is FORGIVEN & BLOOD BOUGHT! Jesus is perfect and yet He died for an imperfect people. His accusation was accurate. He is THE KING! That KING became our Savior. If we receive Jesus and His sacrifice for us, then no longer are we accused of our sin. We are now made right with God and are set free!

*"For He made Him who knew no sin to be sin for us, that we might become the righteousness of God in Him (Jesus)."*
                                    - 2 Corinthians 5:21

Not everyone at the community college agreed with me. I approached an 18 year old young man. As I explained the Gandhi quote and asked what wrong has Jesus done, the man went bezerk! I stood my ground and asked why this man was so hostile to the gospel? Many things were said, but I will never forget his closing remark. He said, "You are trying to talk to me about Jesus being a historical figure. You and I both know that there is so much more to it than that." This teenager knew that Jesus was more than a historical man. He knew that Jesus was really who He said He was!

What God revealed to me later was that this man was afraid. He was afraid of knowing the truth (Romans 1:18). Fear kept him from receiving what Christ had done for him. The 18 year old was not willing to receive the blood of Jesus for his sins. The pain to receive Jesus seemed greater than staying in the current pain of his shame. If only this teenager knew how much God loved him. God knew how much his sin was tearing him up inside. All God wanted to do in that moment was to take it all away. This young man simply couldn't do it. (1 John 4:18-19).

## WHAT IS YOUR RESPONSE?

*"Come now, and let us reason together," says the Lord, "Though your sins are like scarlet,*

*they shall be as white as snow; Though they are red like crimson, they shall be as wool.* **If you are willing and obedient**, *you shall eat the good of the land;* **But if you refuse and rebel**, *you shall be devoured by the sword";* *For the mouth of the Lord has spoken."*

- Isaiah 1:18-20

## WHAT DOES THE BLOOD OF JESUS ACCOMPLISH?

*"How much more shall* **the blood of Christ**, *who through the eternal Spirit offered Himself without spot to God,* **cleanse your conscience from dead works to serve the living God?"**

- Hebrews 9:14

You no longer have to struggle with a guilty mindset. You don't have to feel condemned (Romans 8:1), or worried about being under His wrath and judgment (Romans 1-2). It does not mean that you can continue to deliberately sin whenever you want to (Hebrews 10:26). But it does mean that you are free from a guilty mind once and for all (Hebrews 10:2).

*"But now in Christ Jesus you who once were far off **have been brought near by the blood of Christ.**"*

- Ephesians 2:13

We are brought into relationship with God by the blood of Jesus and not by our good deeds (Romans 5:1).

*"For Christ has not entered the holy places made with hands, which are copies of the true, but into heaven itself, **now to appear in the presence of God for us**; not that He should offer Himself often, as the high priest enters the Most Holy Place every year with blood of another — He then would have had to suffer often since the foundation of the world; but now, once at the end of the ages, **He has appeared to put away sin by the sacrifice of Himself.** And as it is appointed for men to die once, but after this the judgment, so **Christ was offered once to bear the sins of many.** To those who eagerly wait for Him He will appear a second time, apart from sin, for salvation."*

- Hebrews 9:24-28

The blood of Jesus takes away our sins once and for all.

For someone who has never received the blood of Jesus and the sacrifice He has made for their sins, upon receiving Jesus' blood sacrifice, that person is made new and born again! (John 3, 2 Corinthians 5:17). For someone who has already received the blood of Jesus and would consider Him their Lord, how does this chapter apply?

After everything I have written so far, I can still feel distant from God because of the mistakes I make. When I feel God pulling at my heart strings to enter into a time of prayer with Him, I feel gross and separated. I feel like I can't go to Him in boldness so I avoid Him until I "feel like" I can approach Him. The enemy wants to keep us away from God. But receiving the blood of Jesus not only gives us salvation, but it gives us daily relationship and fellowship with God. Look at Hebrews 10:19, 22 – *"Therefore, brethren, having boldness to enter the Holiest **by the blood of Jesus**...let us draw near with a true heart in full assurance of faith, having our **hearts sprinkled from an evil conscience and our bodies washed with pure water."***

Now we can enter into the Presence of God without guilt, shame, or sin because of the blood of Jesus!

*What do you need to conquer*
*and overcome in your life?*

Remember the opening verse of this chapter? The accuser is silenced by the blood of Jesus! Romans 5:8 says, *"God demonstrates His own love toward us, that while we were sinners, Christ died for us."* God says that you are worth it and you are covered.

### APPLICATION

Receive the blood of Jesus and speak the blood of Jesus over your life whenever you are being falsely accused by the enemy. Even if you are being rightly accused by the enemy, the blood of Jesus speaks a better word over your life!

## The seventh weapon of our warfare is the blood of Jesus!

# CONCLUSION

* * *

The purpose of this book was not only to help you live victoriously in your walk with Christ, but it was also meant to make you more aware. I covered 7 spiritual weapons as God gave me inspiration to do so. I didn't even begin to talk about the whole armor of God in Ephesians 6 which includes: the helmet of salvation, the breastplate of righteousness, the belt of truth, the shield of faith, shodded feet with the gospel of peace and the sword of the spirit. (I did cover the last one briefly). I didn't even mention angels or the Name of Jesus itself. I didn't mention the power and authority that Jesus gave us (Luke 10). Nor did I mention the ministry of the Holy Spirit in depth (Acts 1:8). I didn't cover the power of words either (Proverbs 18:21). There are so many more heavenly weapons that are made available to us. My hope is that you find them in the Scriptures and you use them effectively in order to walk freely in Jesus Christ!

In closing I would like to share one more story with you. I was sitting in a coffee shop with a Christian friend of mine. We were talking about God when a lady sat right next to us. We continued our conversation about God and suddenly she chimed in. She began to share matters of spirituality with us, but they did not sound correct. We asked if she believed in Jesus and she replied, "I am a witch." She then began to tell us all about how powerful her group of witches and wiccans are. She boasted about how they are the most powerful group around. She said they pray together and when her group gets together things happen to people. Well, when I went home that night, things began to move in my house. Literally, coat hangers moved. Then my wife started to have horrible dreams. This happened on and off for a few days and when I prayed nothing changed.

Then I was at work one day and my wife called me. She said as she took a nap, she felt attacked in her dreams again. I called my pastor and asked him what I should do. He said to pray and ask God to reveal to you what this type of spirit is. Then my pastor asked me, "What did she say to you?" I told him how she kept telling me how strong her god is. My pastor then said, "If someone is strong, then they don't have to boast about how strong they are." He said, "If she was boasting about her strength, then it really means that she is afraid and weak." I got off the phone, fell on my knees and asked God to reveal to me this type of spirit. The Holy Spirit said to me, "It is a spirit of deception" (1 John 4:1)! The enemy deceived me into thinking that he was stronger than God. I called my wife and told her that it's not what it seems. It's weak and afraid so cast it out! My wife anointed the entire house with oil (Mark 6:13) and we slept peacefully in the house until the day we moved out of it.

I close with this story because the enemy is a liar (John 8:44). God in us is stronger than the enemy in this world (1 John 4:4). Do not let the enemy deceive you and make you think that he is stronger than God in you. The enemy is not stronger. He is weak and afraid and knows his time is short (Revelation 12:12). Pick up your spiritual weapons and use them! You were made to live victoriously in Jesus Christ.

You did not give your life to Jesus in order to live a defeated life. **The enemy has been defeated. Jesus Christ is and always will be victorious** (Revelation 19-20)! Since Jesus is in you, that means that you are made to live victoriously too (Galatians 2:20)!

> *"If you confess with your mouth that Jesus is Lord and believe in your heart that God raised him from the dead, you will be saved. For with the heart one believes and is justified, and with the mouth one confesses and is saved. For the Scripture says, "Everyone who believes in him will not be put to shame."*
>
> - Romans 10:9-11 (ESV)

> *"Yet in all these things we are more than conquerors through Him who loved us."*
>
> - Romans 8:37

## Amen!

# ABOUT THE AUTHOR

Pastor Daniel Aguilar has served in ministry at East River Fellowship in Hillsboro, Oregon, for seven years. His ministry focus has been youth and young adults. Daniel graduated from Multnomah University with degrees in Bible & Theology and Pastoral Ministry. He is married to Sonja Aguilar who graduated from Pacific University and is a dual language kindergarten teacher. They have one son, Joseph, who is in Heaven. Daniel enjoys basketball, art, coffee and walks with his wife.

## Other books by
## Relentless Pursuit Publishing

**62 Reasons to Love the Lord (Vol. 1)**
*This devotional pairs ancient and modern techniques for Biblical meditation so that you can encounter Holy Spirit through the word of God like never before. If you've ever been burned out and overwhelmed by traditional reading plans, this is the devotional for you! Rekindle your love for His word!*

**62 Reasons (Vol. 2)**
*The Healing Scriptures*
*In this volume of 62 Reasons you will be taken on a journey to experience the healing power and presence of God, and receive a fresh revelation and impartation straight from His Word. If you want to immerse yourself in one of the primary ministries of God to and through His people, this is the study for you!*

## Upcoming Titles
*Relentless Pursuit by Keely McCartney*
*What The Bible Says About Healing by Chase McCartney*
*62 Reasons (Vol. 3) by Chase McCartney*

Additional copies of this book and other book titles from Relentless Pursuit Publishing are available online.

Visit us online at
www.relentlesspursuitpublishing.com

"Relentless Pursuit Publishing exists to display the goodness and genius of God through the written word."

Made in the USA
Las Vegas, NV
16 December 2021

38002873R00069